Internet Resource Guide

for use with

Auditing

Ninth Edition

Jack C. Robertson, Ph.D.
Certified Public Accountant
Certified Fraud Examiner
C. T. Zlatkovich Centennial Professor of Accounting
The University of Texas at Austin

Timothy J. Louwers, Ph.D.
Certified Public Accountant
Certified Internal Auditor
Assistant Professor of Accounting
Louisiana State University

Boston   Burr Ridge, IL   Dubuque, IA   Madison, WI   New York   San Francisco   St. Louis
Bangkok   Bogotá   Caracas   Lisbon   London   Madrid
Mexico City   Milan   New Delhi   Seoul   Singapore   Sydney   Taipei   Toronto

Irwin/McGraw-Hill

A Division of The McGraw-Hill Companies

Internet Resource Guide for use with
AUDITING

Copyright ©1999 by The McGraw-Hill Companies, Inc. All rights reserved.
Printed in the United States of America.
The contents of, or parts thereof, may be reproduced for use with
AUDITING
Jack C. Robertson and Timothy J. Louwers
provided such reproductions bear copyright notice and may not be reproduced in
any form for any other purpose without permission of the publisher.

3 4 5 6 7 8 9 0 CUS/CUS 9 3 2 1 0 9

ISBN 0-07-365650-X

http://www.mhhe.com

TABLE OF CONTENTS

INTRODUCTION 1

   1. Professional Practice 5
   2. Audit and Attestation Standards and Assurance Services 13
   3. Reports on Audited Financial Statements 15
   4. Audit Objectives, Procedures, and Working Papers 17
   5. Audit Planning with Analytical Procedures, Risk, and Materiality 18
   6. Internal Control Evaluation: Assessing Control Risk 22
   7. Audit Sampling 24
   8. Fraud Awareness Auditing: SAS No. 82 and Beyond 25
   9. Revenue and Collection Cycle 31
  10. Acquisition and Expenditure Cycle 33
  11. Production and Payroll Cycle 36
  12. Finance and Investment Cycle 37
  13. Completing the Audit 40

  A. Test of Controls with Attribute Sampling 41
  B. Test of Balances with Dollar-Value Sampling 41
  C. Auditing in an Electronic Environment 42
  D. Information System Auditing 44
  E. Other Public Accounting Services and Reports 46
  F. Operational Auditing: Governmental and Internal Audits 48
  G. Professional Ethics 51
  H. Legal Liability 53

Appendix A: Other Cool Internet Stuff 55
Appendix B: Other Accounting Sites 56

> *A journey of a thousand sites begins with a single click.*
>
> -Anonymous Internet commentator

Introduction

The advent of the Internet has been likened to the invention of the airplane or the discovery of electricity-- it has opened new worlds previously unattainable through traditional means. For example, you can send e-mail messages quicker than it takes to walk to your mailbox. You can visit foreign lands through your computer terminal without ever leaving the comfort of your own home. Forget to send off that credit card payment that is due tomorrow? No worries-- you can pay your bills virtually instantaneously through electronic funds transfers. The Internet also provides an incredible library of information that you can access without ever having to ask where the library building is.

A Brief History

The Internet was created as part of a Department of Defense initiative in the late 1960s/early 1970s as a means of linking computers to facilitate communications during wartime conditions. Later, as the technology linking the network of computers became declassified, the National Science Foundation (NSF) created its own network of linked computers (NSFNet) to allow researchers to share academic research. Due to funding limitations, however, the network was turned over to commercial interests. As technology continued to expand, the services provided were upgraded from early text-only communications to include multimedia graphics presentations that now include real-time sound and video.

As of 1998, the Internet has grown to include over 100 million users on over 30,000 computer networks. This figure is estimated to grow approximately 10% per month!

FAQs (Frequently Asked Questions)

What exactly is the Internet?

The **Internet** is a global network of electronically linked computers that allows users to access information stored on computers (**servers**) located almost anywhere in the world. The Internet is also a global communications medium. For example, you can "talk" to other Internet users in foreign countries via e-mail. Individuals can access newspaper articles from around the world from across the world. In addition, more and more companies are using the Internet to advertise goods and services. The Internet provides a new means of access to clients, suppliers, and business partners. For example, there is an Internet site established for individuals who are moving (http://www.homefair.com) that allows people to view apartments and real estate in the city to which they are planning to move. Information is also easily accessible. Once you've located the site that you are interested in, information is available at the click of a mouse button.

The Internet Protocol (IP) provides the "rules of the road" for the "information superhighway." Each computer on the Internet has a unique IP address consisting of up to five numbers (each less than 256) separated by periods (e.g., 12.22.16.25.9). Information is transferred from computer to computer in "byte-sized" pieces of less than 1,500 bytes. By keeping the packets relatively small, no one person can monopolize the network.

> *Give a man a fish and you feed him for a day; teach him to use the Net and he won't bother you for weeks.*
>
> -Anonymous Internet Commentator

What kinds of stuff can you find on the Internet?

Most computer users in the industrialized areas of the world may observe, or **browse**, data stored on the Internet at a relatively low cost. While the Internet is criticized for being vast, disorganized, and confusing, it provides excellent opportunities in communication, education, commerce, and entertainment. The Internet provides an incredible assortment of information that can be easily accessed. For example, the Internet contains the following:

1. **Documents.** The Internet provides articles, magazines, newspapers, books, and information on almost any subject that you have interest. You can also find airline schedules, access your bank's records in order to balance your checkbook, or check out the prices of used automobiles.

2. **Software.** The Internet is a great source for information on software upgrades and free software programs (shareware). Many companies are willing to allow you to test-drive their programs in hopes that you will purchase upgrades for the software if you like it.

3. **Communication.** The Internet also provides a place to interact with other Internet users who may share common interests. There are bulletin boards that provide useful information on specific topics. Another means of communication is through "chat groups" that allow Internet users to communicate directly through their computers on a real-time basis. Finally, there are listserves that send out messages that have been posted to those individuals who have requested it. For example, software is available that notifies you when a web site has changed.

How can I access information on the Internet?

You can access information on the Internet through a variety of means. The three primary means are:

1. **Telnet** allows you to log onto other computer systems from a remote location through telecommunication lines via a modem. When logged on through telnet, you can use your own keyboard as if it were connected directly to the remote computer.

2. **File Transfer Protocol (FTP)** allows you to move files to and from remote computers. You may transfer files even though the computer systems are dissimilar. For example, you can transfer files between an IBM mainframe computer and your personal computer with ease.

3. The graphics segment of the Internet is called the **World Wide Web**. Information on the Internet is typically stored in **web sites** maintained on various servers. Most information on the Web is displayed in a series of screens with graphic icons known as **links.** Most web sites are written in HyperText Markup Language (HTML). By clicking on the links, you may gain access to other screens in the hypertext format.

There's no place like http://www.home.com.

-Anonymous Internet commentator

Tell me more about Web sites

The **home page** of a web site is the primary screen of a web site that usually provides guidance to other information provided in the web site. Each page in a web site is identified by a unique address known as a **uniform resource locator** (URL) such as the one that follows:

```
Interpretive      Server                    File Location
Language          Location                  Within the Server
   ┌──┐  ┌──────────────────┐         ┌──────────────────────┐
   http://www.mhhe.com/business/accounting/Robertson
```

The address contains three parts:

- The first part identifies the interpretive language. As noted earlier, most web sites are written in HyperText Markup Language that is accessed, processed, and translated using HyperText Transfer Protocol (HTTP).

- The second part of the URL identifies the server that stores the information. Servers have unique addresses most commonly beginning with "www" (for World Wide Web), a unique company or organizational identifier, and suffix representing the type of organization that is sponsoring the server. Some common suffixes for U.S. web sites include ".edu" for educational institution, ".com" for company, and ".org" for organization. Other countries also have their own unique suffixes (e.g., ".uk" for United Kingdom, "cn" for China, etc.). Because of the incredible explosion of Internet servers, the number of identifying suffixes are being expanded to provide more accurate descriptions of Internet server sponsors.

- Finally, the file on the server in which the data is contained is identified in the last part of the URL.

How do I find what I am looking for on the Internet?

Some of the Internet's most powerful tools are **search engines**. Search engines comb millions of web sites looking for key words that you have specified. For example, after the popularity of the movie *Titanic*, over 100 web sites were devoted to its leading man Leonardo DiCaprio, all of which would show up in a search using his first and last names as the key words. The most widely used search engines can be found at the following URL's:

1. AltaVista — http://www.altavista.com
2. Excite — http://www.excite.com
3. Infoseek — http://www.infoseek.com
4. Lycos — http://www.lycos.com
5. Yahoo! — http://www.yahoo.com
6. Webcrawler — http://www.webcrawler.com

Not all search engines are alike. A recent article cited in the Wall Street Journal (April 10, 1998) noted that the various search engines covered from 10 - 34% of the Web. Further, search results not only differ, but the search engines present them differently. Try each search engine until you feel comfortable with one. Use the other search engines as backups if you are not finding what you are looking for or to expand your search results.

How does the Internet affect the auditing profession?

We're glad you asked this last question! In fact, this Internet Resource Guide was written specifically because there are so many implications for the auditing profession. In this supplement, we will explore the Internet together examining new sources of information that will be useful to you should you choose a career in auditing.

> "We've heard that a million monkeys at a million keyboards could produce the Complete Works of Shakespeare. Now, thanks to the Internet, we know this is not true."
>
> -Robert Wilensky, University of California

Chapter 1: Professional Practice

The United States is one of the few countries whose financial reporting standards are promulgated by the private sector rather than the government. This private sector responsibility has led the United States' accounting profession to be recognized as the world leader in the development of accounting policy. One of the consequences of the private sector responsibility is the large number of organizations that are involved in standard setting, including the American Institute of CPAs (AICPA), the Financial Accounting Standards Board (FASB), the Governmental Accounting Standards Board (GASB), and the Securities and Exchange Commission (SEC). The textbook devotes much time and space to the discussion of these various accounting standards setting groups that regulate the U.S. accounting profession. Unfortunately, due to limitations of the publishing business, we are not always able to address the new and exciting things that are happening in our profession as often as we would like. Instead we suggest that you check out the information at the source.

Exercise 1.1: Links to the Professional Organizations

Visit each of the following links on the following pages to find out the most recent happenings in the accounting profession from the following organizations.

1. Securities and Exchange Commission (SEC)

2. American Institute of Certified Public Accountants (AICPA)

3. Financial Accounting Standards Board (FASB)

4. Governmental Accounting Standards Board (GASB)

5. National Association of State Boards of Accountancy (NASBA)

Securities and Exchange Commission (SEC)
Established by Congress under the Securities Exchange Act of 1934, the Securities and Exchange Commission (SEC) is an independent, nonpartisan, quasi-judicial regulatory agency, charged with the responsibility of administering the federal securities laws. The purpose of these laws (and of the SEC) is to "protect investors in securities markets that operate fairly and to ensure that investors have access to disclosure of all material information concerning publicly traded securities." The SEC also regulates firms engaged in the purchase or sale of securities, people who provide investment advice, and investment companies. From the SEC Web site, you can learn more about the SEC, obtain summaries of recent legislation affecting the accounting community, and access corporate filings with the SEC. You can also access the SEC's EDGAR (Electronic Data Gathering, Analysis and Retrieval) database directly from this site. We will explore the EDGAR database in Chapter 3.

http://www.sec.gov

American Institute of Certified Public Accountants
With over 300,000 members, the AICPA is the leading professional association for CPAs in the United States. The AICPA provides a myriad of services and products that allow CPAs to continue to provide high quality client service. Because the Auditing Standards Board is part of the AICPA, the site also provides links to review summaries of proposed auditing standards or to download complete copies of exposure drafts.

http://www.aicpa.org

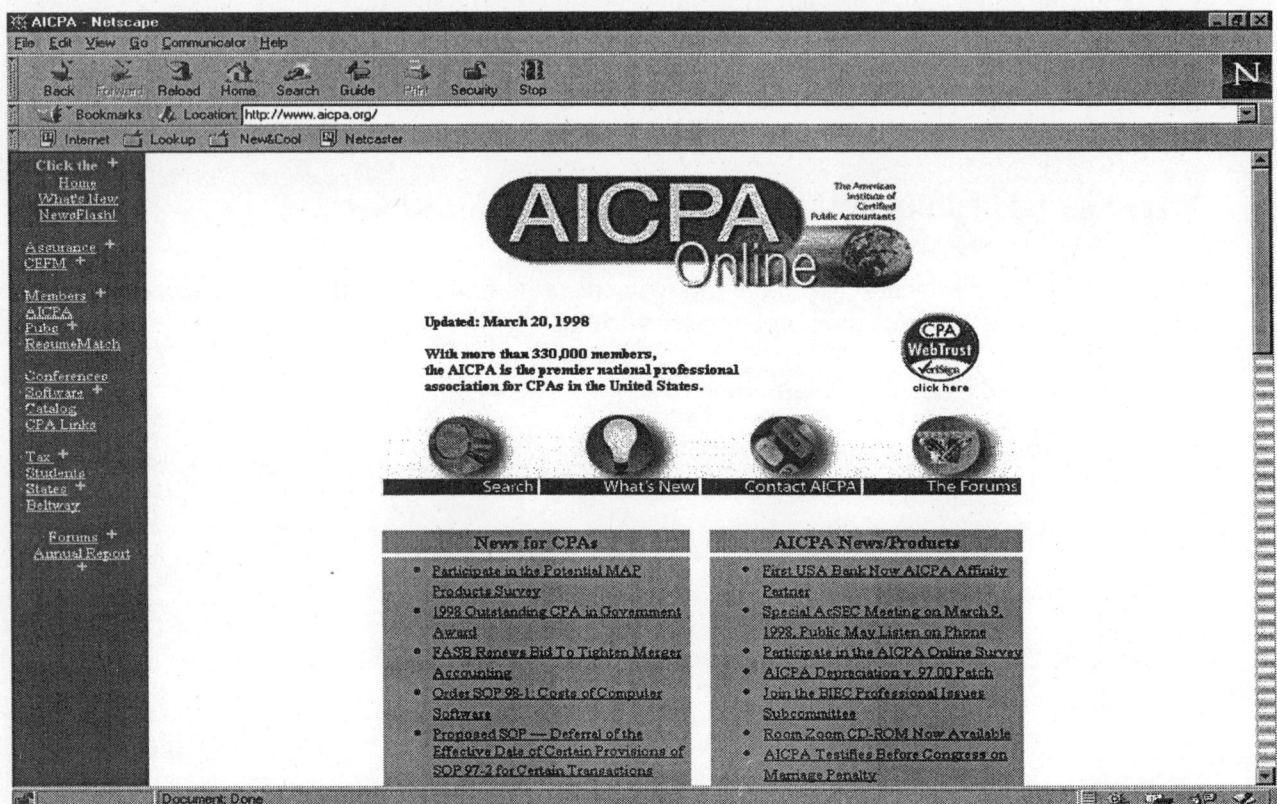

What is most recent Statement on Auditing Standards (SAS) issued by the Auditing Standards Board?

Permission to include the contents page image of the AICPA website was obtained from the AICPA.

Financial Accounting Standards Board

The Financial Accounting Standards Board was established in 1973 "to establish and improve standards of financial accounting and reporting for the guidance and education of the public, including issuers, auditors and users of financial information." From the FASB Web site, you can obtain summaries of existing Statements of Financial Accounting Standards (SFAS), download exposure drafts of those being considered, and get recent press clippings of FASB activities.

http://www.rutgers.edu/accounting/raw/fasb

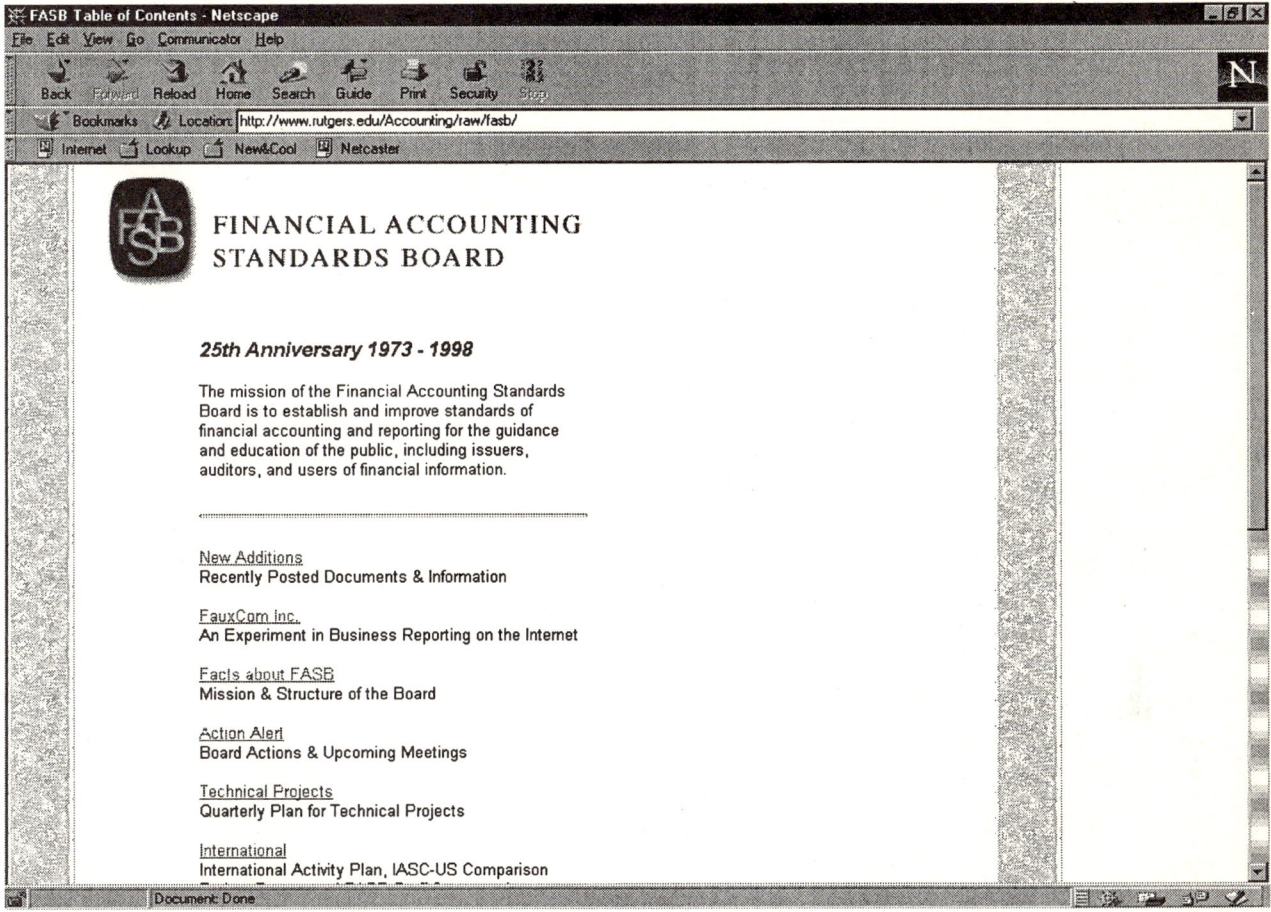

What is the most recent Statement of Financial Accounting Standards (SFAS) issued by the FASB?

Permission to include the contents page image of the FASB and GASB websites was obtained from the Financial Accounting Standards Board and the Governmental Accounting Standards Board.

Governmental Accounting Standards Board

The Financial Accounting Foundation organized the Governmental Accounting Standards Board (GASB) in 1984 "to establish standards of financial accounting and reporting for state and local governmental entities." From the GASB Web site, you can obtain summaries of existing Statements of Governmental Accounting Standards, download exposure drafts of those being considered, and get recent press clippings of GASB activities.

http://www.gasb.org

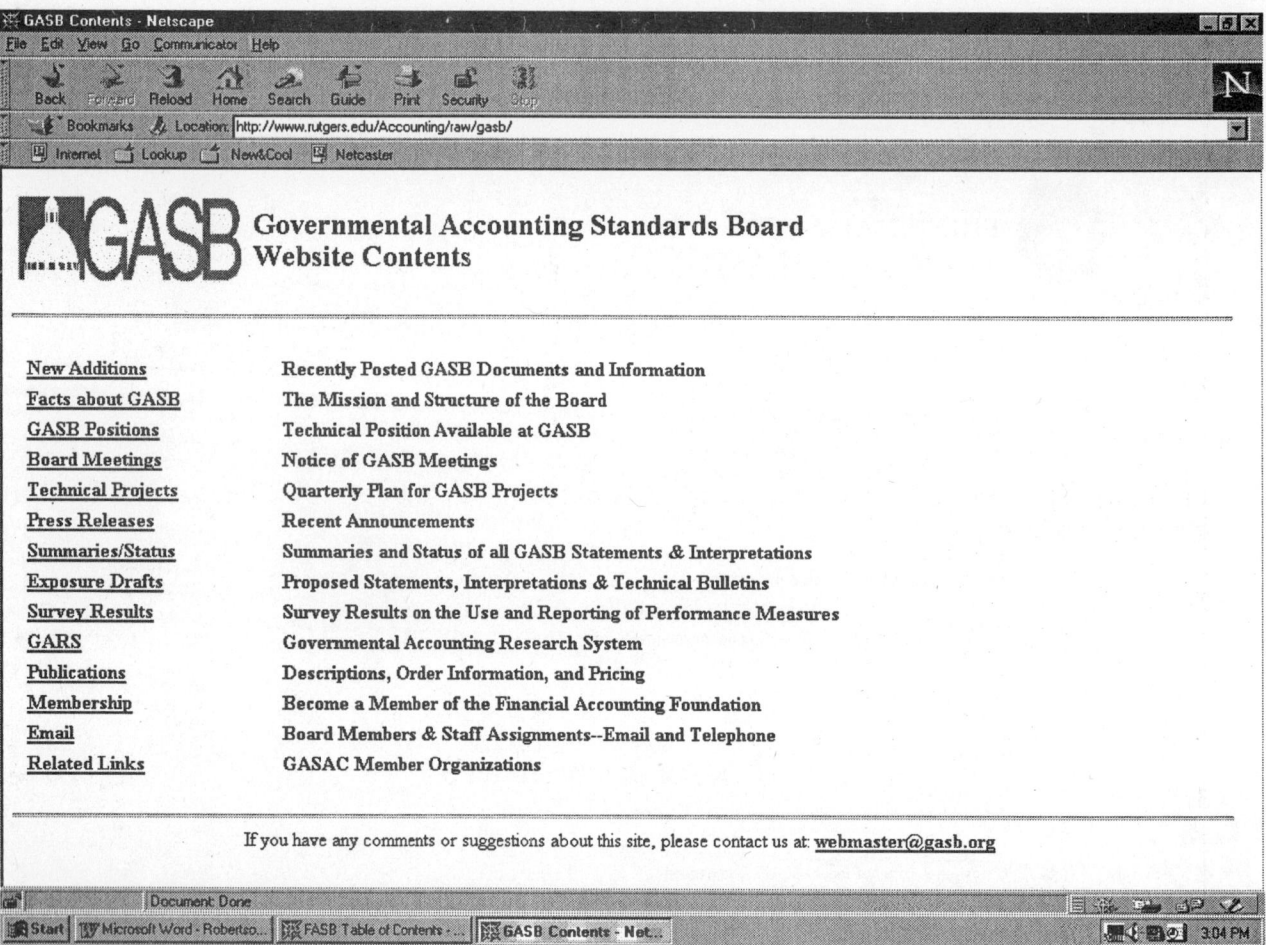

What is the most recent GASB statement issued?

Permission to include the contents page image of the FASB and GASB websites was obtained from the Financial Accounting Standards Board and the Governmental Accounting Standards Board.

Exercise 1.2: Visit the AICPA!

The American Institute of CPAs provides the primary means of professional support for most practicing CPAs. Visit the AICPA web site and find 5 ways that the AICPA can help CPAs continue to provide quality service to their clients.

http://www.aicpa.org

1.

2.

3.

4.

5.

List five products or services that the AICPA provides to students at little of no cost and provide a brief description of each.

1.

2.

3.

4.

5.

Exercise 1.3: Professional Certification

As mentioned in the text, each state has unique rules for certification concerning education, work experience, and residency. Visit the web site for your state board of accountancy and download a list of the requirements for becoming a CPA in your state. Although not all of the state boards of accountancy have web sites, you might be able to find your state's web site by accessing the National Association of State Boards of Accountancy (NASBA) at its web site:

http://www.nasba.org

Experience requirements?	
Education requirements?	
Residency requirements?	

Exercise 1.4: 150 Hours by the Year 2000?

The AICPA has strongly suggested that each state require CPA candidates to have at least 150 hours of education before sitting for the CPA Examination. From the AICPA's web site, find out how many states have adopted the AICPA's guideline of 150 hours of education.

http://www.aicpa.org

How many states have enacted legislation with respect to the 150-hour requirement? _____

Of the states that have enacted legislation on the 150-hour requirement, …

    how many states require the 150-hours now? _____

    how many states will require the 150 hours at a future date? _____

Exercise 1.5: Visit Some Accounting Firms!

Harcourt Brace Professional Publishing (HBPP) hosts a site that identifies and provides links to exceptional accounting firm Internet sites. Most CPA firm sites include a description of the firm that details the firm's history and personnel. In addition, almost every firm provided a means of contacting firm members by e-mail. Surprisingly, many of the firms do not provide detailed descriptions of the services they offer or the physical location of the firm. From the links on the HBPP site (**http://www.hbpp.com/topfive/tf_archive.html**), visit five accounting firms' sites and check the features that each firm provides.

What do firms put on the Internet?

	Firm 1	Firm 2	Firm 3	Firm 4	Firm 5
Firm Name					
E-Mail Addresses to Contact the Firm					
Description of the Firm - "Who Are We?"					
Identification of Services Offered by the Firm					
Location of the Firm					
Links to Sources Outside the Firm					
Profiles of Firm Members					
Statement of the Firm Philosophy or Mission					
Tax or Business Tip of the Day/Month/Week					
Employment Opportunities Within the Firm					
On-Line Newsletter					
Guest Book (for Client Leads)					
Products/Literature Offered by the Firm					
Description of Seminars Offered by the Firm					
Newsletter Subscription Information					
Calendar of Important Tax Dates					
Invitation to "Ask the Expert"					
Counter of the Number of Site Visitors					
Comments or Testimonials from Clients					
Internet Links to Clients					
Humor and Entertainment					
Disclaimers					

Chapter 2: Audit and Attestation Standards and Assurance Services

Exercise 2.1: GAAS and the Internet

Chapter 2 includes a discussion of the 10 Generally Accepted Auditing Standards (GAAS). What are the implications of the Internet on an auditor's adherence to GAAS? How do the general standards of generally accepted auditing standards apply to the auditor's (or client's) use of the Internet? field work standards? reporting standards?

To find the answer to this question, we suggest that you check out a brief discussion of this issue under "Hot Topics" contained on our Internet Site:

http://www.mhhe.com/business/accounting/robertson

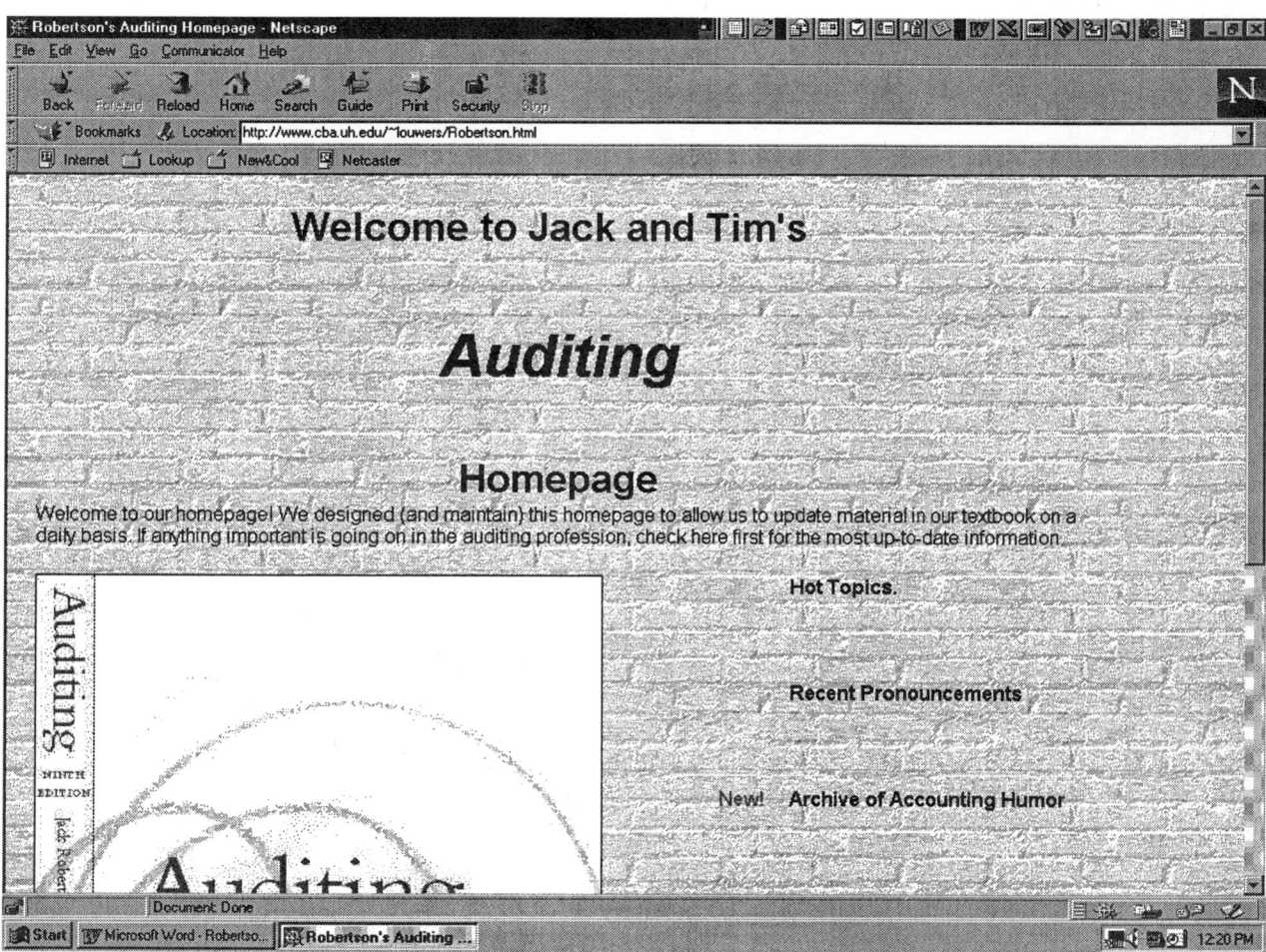

Exercise 2.2: Independence and the Independence Standards Board (ISB)

Given the auditor's role of watchdog to safeguard public interests, the importance of independence can not be underestimated. Despite its importance, there are several unresolved issues relating to current independence rules and practices. For example, the SEC and the AICPA have different independence rules. Second, critics of the current system have argued that the AICPA independence rules have evolved in a piecemeal fashion, not linked to any underlying principles. Critics have also expressed concern that the current rules reflect some outdated assumptions. Finally, regulators were finding it difficult to reconcile U.S. and foreign independence rules.

To resolve these issues, the AICPA created an Independence Standards Board in 1997 to develop a conceptual framework that will facilitate the promulgation of principle-based standards and to develop a process for addressing emerging independence issues.

http://www.aicpa.org/members/div/secps/index.htm

After visiting the site, answer the following questions:

1. How much progress has the ISB made since its inception in 1997?	
2. What resources are available through the ISB to resolve independence-related issues?	

Chapter 3: Reports on Audited Financial Statements

One of the great resources on the World Wide Web for auditors is the SEC's EDGAR system. EDGAR stands for Electronic Data Gathering, Analysis and Retrieval system. Most publicly traded companies file SEC-required documents electronically. The SEC makes this information available on the its web page. Some of the more useful filings for accountants include the following:

Form	Description
Annual Report to Shareholders	The Annual Report to Shareholders is the principal document used by most public companies to disclose corporate information to shareholders. It usually includes financial data, results of continuing operations, market segment information, new product plans, subsidiary activities and research and development activities. Sometimes, companies include the annual report by reference in their Form 10-K filed with the SEC, and the actual report may not be present.
Form 10-K or 10-KSB	This is the annual report that most reporting companies file with the Commission. It provides a comprehensive overview of the registrant's business. The report must be filed within 90 days after the end of the company's fiscal year.
Form 10-Q	The Form 10-Q is a report filed quarterly by most reporting companies. It includes unaudited financial statements and provides a continuing view of the company's financial position during the year. The report must be filed for each of the first three fiscal quarters of the company's fiscal year and is due within 45 days of the close of the quarter.
Form 8-K	This is the "current report" that is used to report the occurrence of any material events or corporate changes which are of importance to investors or security holders and previously have not been reported by the registrant. It provides more current information on certain specified events than would Forms 10-Q or 10-K.
Form S-1	This is the basic registration form used to register public securities offerings.

Exercise 3.1: Look up some annual reports

Choose ten publicly traded companies with which you are familiar. After accessing the EDGAR database, download copies of the auditors' reports from the Form 10-K filings and check the boxes in the table below that apply. The first has been done for you. (*Hint:* Search the 10-K filings. Once you've accessed the 10-K filing, use the "Find in page" function in your Internet browser to locate the auditor's report using the key words "auditor" or "accountant.")

http://www.sec.gov/

Company Name	Type of Opinion				Additional Explanatory Paragraph?		
	Unqualified Opinion	Qualified Opinion	Disclaimer of Opinion	Adverse Opinion	Consistency	Going Concern	Emphasize a matter
Universal Seismic (1997)	✓					✓	

Chapter 4: Audit Objectives, Procedures, and Working Papers

The Internet provides a great deal of support for practicing accountants. For example, auditors often get together to share best practices. There are two sites that list audit programs for a number of different audit areas. If you need an audit program, you can simply access one of the sites, download a program, and modify it to meet the needs of your client's engagement.

Exercise 4.1: Audit Programs

Listed below are web sites that allow an auditor to download copies of audit programs. Access one of the sites, browse through the programs, and download an audit program that interests you.

Auditors Sharing Audit Programs (ASAP)

<http://users.aol.com/auditnet/asap_ind.htm>

or

<ftp://ftp.unf.edu/pub/auditnet/programs>

(**Note:** Do not use the "HTTP://" prefix when you attempt to access this site.)

Chapter 5: Audit Planning with Analytical Procedures, Risk, and Materiality

As discussed in the textbook, auditors use analytical procedures quite extensively as an efficient means of planning, conducting, and reviewing the audit engagement. The Internet provides great resources to assist in the analytical procedure process by making hundreds of company's financial statements available for comparison purposes. Below are some sources of company information that you can access for comparison purposes.

Hoovers on-line ("The Ultimate Source for Company Information")

<u>http://www.hoovers.com</u>

Disclosure Company ("The First Source for Financial Intelligence")

<u>http://www.disclosure.com</u>

SEC's EDGAR Database

<u>http://www.sec.gov/</u>

Additionally, auditors are able to find significant industry information in the following locations:

CNN Financial Network

<u>http://cnnfn.com</u>

Department of Commerce

<u>http://www.doc.gov</u>

Wall Street Journal

<u>http://interactive.wsj.com</u>

Exercise 5.1: Analytical Procedures

Before accepting a new client, it is important to determine how that company is doing in comparison to its competitors and its industry. Once the client has been accepted, analytical procedures are useful to identify areas of risk that may require a heightened sense of awareness of potential problems.

Calculate the following ratios for Kingston Company and compare them to those of its major competitors.

	Kingston	Lowe's	Home Depot	Payless Cashways
Common-Size Data				
Gross Profit/Sales				
Net Income/Sales				
Current Assets/Total Assets				
Current Liabilities/Total Assets				
Liabilities/Total Assets				
Equity/Total Assets				
Ratio Analysis				
Days' Sales in Accounts Receivable				
Days' Sales in Inventory				
Accounts Receivable Turnover Ratio				
Inventory Turnover Ratio				
Return on Assets				
Return on Equity				
Current Ratio				
Quick Ratio				
Times Interest Earned				

What inferences can you make from your comparisons? What areas appear to be of concern? Write a brief planning memo discussing your findings.

Exercise 5.2: Analytical Procedures

Suppose a potential client in the footwear industry has approached your firm. Its two main competitors are Nike and Reebok. After calculating the company's ratios, you decide to compare the ratios with those of its competitors and its industry.

	Client	Nike	Reebok	Industry
Common-Size Data				
Gross Profit/Sales	38%			39%
Net Income/Sales	10%			10%
Current Assets/Total Assets	96%			74%
Current Liabilities/Total Assets	60%			34%
Liabilities/Total Assets	68%			41%
Equity/Total Assets	32%			59%
Ratio Analysis				
Days' Sales in Accounts Receivable	81 days			60 days
Days' Sales in Inventory	190 days			65 days
Accounts Receivable Turnover Ratio	4.5 times			6.6 times
Inventory Turnover Ratio	1.9 times			4.1 times
Return on Assets	17%			17%
Return on Equity	53%			29%
Current Ratio	1.6 : 1			2 : 1
Quick Ratio	0.7 : 1			1 : 1
Times Interest Earned	16 times			16 times

What inferences can you make from your comparisons? What areas appear to be of concern? Write a brief planning memo discussing your findings.

Exercise 5.3: Industry Risk Assessment

Industry risk assessment is another critical part of planning. The company can not be viewed as a stand-alone entity. Instead, it must be viewed in the context of the industry in which it participates. For example, a company may remain stable in terms of revenues. If the rest of the industry is booming, however, revenue stability becomes a negative factor in the company's business risk assessment. Similarly, if competitors are facing high degrees of litigation involving environmental issues, the auditor must be aware of the potential for litigation affecting the client's operations.

Imagine that you are the "in-charge" auditor for a startup client in the industry of your choosing – entertainment, sports, footwear, hotel, etc. Perform a search looking for industry trends, number and size of competitors, and industry prospects.

Write a brief memo to the partner-in-charge describing your findings. Mention such factors as:

1. Overall industry market.

2. Stage of industry (developing, mature, etc.),

3. Industry competition,

4. Industry-specific reporting practices (if any), and

5. Industry-specific risks.

Conclude your memo with an industry classification (high, medium, or low). Based on your classification, how would you modify your audit approach to address the industry risk level? (Charge higher/lower fees? Assign more/less experienced personnel? Obtain outside expertise?)

Chapter 6: Internal Control Evaluation: Assessing Control Risk

Assignment 6.1: SAS No. 78 versus SAS No. 55

Statement of Auditing Standard (SAS) No. 78 revised the definition and description of internal control contained in SAS No. 55, "Consideration of the Internal Control Structure in a Financial Statement Audit," to recognize the definition and description contained in "Internal Control Integrated Framework," published by the Committee of Sponsoring Organizations of the Treadway Commission (the COSO report). This statement is one of the most important SAS's to have been issued in the past decade. Unfortunately, your partner-in-charge is unfamiliar with the Statement and has asked that you prepare a brief memo on the changes from SAS No. 55 to SAS No. 78.

Access the AICPA web site to find a summary of SAS No. 78 and write a brief memo explaining the new definition of internal control and the changes in terminology from SAS No. 55 to SAS No. 78. (**Hint:** SAS No. 78 describes the changes from the previous SAS.)

http://www.aicpa.org

Assignment 6.2: Internal Control Questionnaire

The Internet provides a great deal of support for practicing accountants. For example, auditors often get together to share best practices. There are two sites that list audit programs for a number of different audit areas. If you need an audit program, you can simply access one of the sites, download a program, and modify it to meet the needs of your client's engagement.

Access one of the **Auditors Sharing Audit Programs (ASAP)** sites to download a copy of an internal control questionnaire. Save the program and import it into a word processing program. Modify the program for use in the Kingston Company audit engagement.

Auditors Sharing Audit Programs (ASAP)

http://users.aol.com/auditnet/asap_ind.htm

or

ftp.unf.edu/pub/auditnet/programs

(**Note:** Do not use the "HTTP://" prefix when you attempt to access this site.)

(**Hint:** Be sure to read and study the background information about Kingston Company at the end of Chapter 4, the corporate minutes (5.18), and materials at the end of Chapter 6. You need to know about the company in order to modify an existing audit program. Do the best you can with the available information.)

Chapter 7: Audit Sampling

Exercise 7.1: New International Sampling Standard?

As of the publication of this document, the International Auditing Practices Committee (IAPC) of the International Federation of Accountants (IFAC) recently released, for exposure, a revision of Audit Sampling and Other Selective Testing Procedures, International Standard on Auditing (ISA) 530. Access the IFAC's web site and answer the questions below.

International Federation of Accountants (IFAC)

<big>http://www.ifac.org/</big>

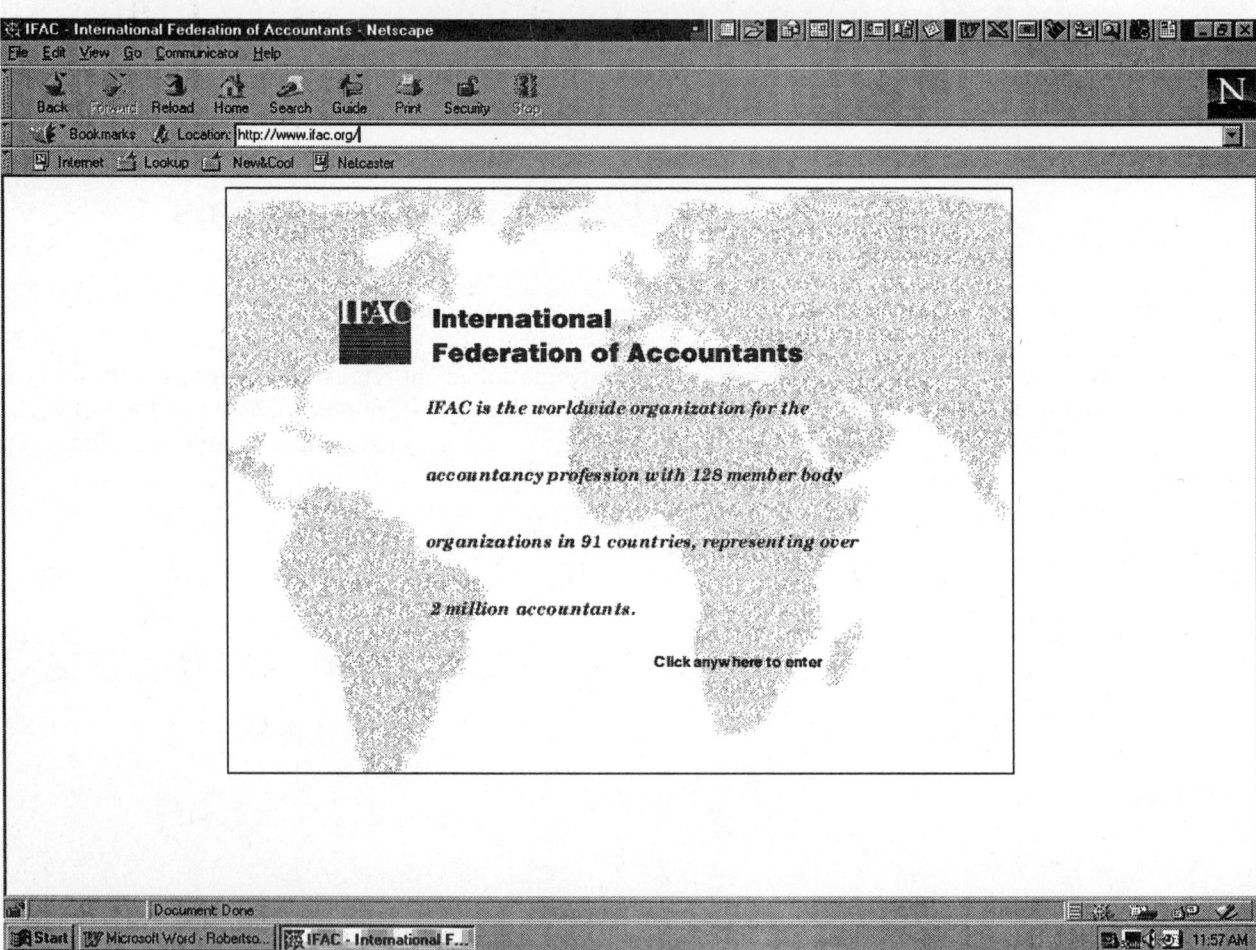

Why was the revision considered necessary? What are some of the major points of the revision? Has a new standard been issued yet?

Permission to include the cover page image of the IFAC website was obtained from the International Federation of Accountants.

Chapter 8: Fraud Awareness Auditing: SAS No. 82 and Beyond

One of the biggest obstacles in fraud auditing is obtaining timely information to effectively prevent and detect fraud. The Internet is a great place to find resources for fraud auditing. We have listed several web sites below that you might find interesting:

American College of Forensic Investigators: http://www.acfe.com

American Institute of CPAs (AICPA): http://www.aicpa.org/

Association of Certified Fraud Examiners (ACFE): http://www.acfe.org

Better Business Bureau: http://www.bbb.org

Business Software Alliance: http://ww.bsa.org

Check Information Systems:
http://www.angelfire.com/biz/BOGUS/index.html

Criminal Justice Links: http://www.fsu.edu/~crimdo/cj.html

Federal Trade Commission: http://www.ftc.gov

Index to Private Investigators: http://www.echotech.com/pi.htm

Internal Revenue Service: http://www.irs.ustreas.com

Investigative Research of Boston: http://world.std.com/~mmoore

Law Enforcement Links: http://www.leolinks.com

Legal Information Institute:
http://www.law.cornell.edu/topics/index?

National Check Fraud Center:
http://ww.angelfire.com/biz/NCFC/index.html

National Fraud Information Center: **http://www.fraud.org**

PI Mall: **http://www.pimall.com**

US Securities and Exchange Commission: **http://www.sec.gov**

In addition to the above sites, the **Governmental Accounting Office (GAO)** maintains a publication entitled "Investigator's Guide to Sources of Information" compiled by its Office of Special Investigations. It contains citations of numerous databases on people, property, business, and finance. It is accessible at **http://www.gao.gov**.

Exercise 8.1: Cite the Site

From the sites listed on the previous pages, where would you find...

a. Information on the latest scams involving check forgery?

b. A listing of private investigators specializing in computer crime?

c. Information on software piracy?

d. Information on how to become a Certified Fraud Examiner (CFE)?

e. Business and consumer alerts about fraudulent activity?

f. Government resources to aid fraud investigation?

Exercise 8.2: Certified Fraud Examiner Requirements

Access the Association of Fraud Examiners to find out the requirements for becoming a Certified Fraud Examiner.

http://www.acfe.org

List the requirements below:

Experience requirements?	
Education requirements?	
Exam requirements?	

Permission to include the contents page image of the ACFE website was obtained from the Association of Certified Fraud Examiners.

Exercise 8.3: SAS No. 82

The AICPA has devoted space on its web page for information on SAS No. 82: "Consideration of Fraud in a Financial Statement Audit."

http://www.aicpa.org

List the resources that the AICPA provides on its Internet site on this subject.

Exercise 8.4: Do a Background Check on the Internet

Many important public documents (lawsuits, judgments, bankruptcy filings, and liens) are now stored electronically on servers that can be accessed via the Internet. One company (**KnowX**) provides searches of these documents at little or no cost (depending on the time of day and the extent of the search).

Access the KnowX site and perform a free search. Your search may be on a parent, guardian, or a long-lost friend. You can also perform a search on yourself to find out what information is available about you that others can find. Alternatively, you can perform a search on a public figure (politician, movie star, etc.). Write a report of all the flags you find in public records.

KnowX: **http//:www.knowx.com**

CAUTION: Although these are public records, the information contained in the records may be of a sensitive nature. If you a performing a search on someone that you know personally, we **strongly suggest** that you contact your target person for permission before actually conducting the search.

Chapter 9: Revenue and Collection Cycle

Exercise 9.1: Revenue Cycle Audit Program

The Internet provides a great deal of support for practicing accountants. For example, auditors often get together to share best practices. There are two sites that list audit programs for a number of different audit areas. If you need an audit program, you can simply access one of the sites, download a program, and modify it to meet the needs of your client's engagement.

Access one of the **Auditors Sharing Audit Programs (ASAP)** sites and download a revenue cycle audit program. Save the program and import it into a word processing software program. Modify the program for use in the Kingston Company audit engagement.

Auditors Sharing Audit Programs (ASAP)

http://users.aol.com/auditnet/asap_ind.htm

or

ftp.unf.edu/pub/auditnet/programs

(**Note:** Do not use the "HTTP://" prefix when you attempt to access this site.)

(**Hint:** Be sure to read and study the background information about Kingston Company at the end of Chapter 4, the corporate minutes (5.18), and materials at the end of Chapter 6. You need to know about the company in order to modify an existing audit program. Do the best you can with the available information.)

Exercise 9.2: Customer Verification

Kingston Company is one of your clients. Before sending out confirmations to Kingston's customers, you want to verify that the customers are real and that their addresses are correct.

Customer	Address	Web Site	Comments?
ADM Company	126 La Grange P.O. Box 74 Red Wing, MN 55066-2317		
E. T. Horn Company	16141 Heron Ave. La Mirada, CA 90638		
Paint, Inc.	6007 Highland Rd. Baton Rouge, LA 70810		
Ribelin Sales, Inc.	3857 Miller Park Drive P.O. Box 461673 Garland, TX 75046		
Seegott Inc.	10040 Aurora-Hudson Rd Streetsboro, OH 44241		
Tarr, Inc.	2429 North Borthwick P.O. Box 12570 Portland, OR 97212		
Tarr and Futhers Paint Supplies	14072 Corporate Blvd. West Palm Beach, FL 33414		

Hint: Some of these distributors are real, some are not. Search the web to find web sites for the real suppliers.

Chapter 10: Acquisition and Expenditure Cycle

Exercise 10.1: Expenditure Cycle Audit Program

The Internet provides a great deal of support for practicing accountants. For example, auditors often get together to share best practices. There are two sites that list audit programs for a number of different audit areas. If you need an audit program, you can simply access one of the sites, download a program, and modify it to meet the needs of your client's engagement.

Access one of the **Auditors Sharing Audit Programs (ASAP)** sites and download an expenditure cycle audit program. Save the program and import it into a word processing software program. Modify the program for use in the Kingston Company audit engagement.

Auditors Sharing Audit Programs (ASAP)

http://users.aol.com/auditnet/asap_ind.htm

or

ftp.unf.edu/pub/auditnet/programs

(**Note:** Do not use the "HTTP://" prefix when you attempt to access this site.)

(**Hint:** Be sure to read and study the background information about Kingston Company at the end of Chapter 4, the corporate minutes (5.18), and materials at the end of Chapter 6. You need to know about the company in order to modify an existing audit program. Do the best you can with the available information.)

Exercise 10.2: Valuation

One of your clients is Slimey's Used Cars. The owner is applying for a loan to expand his lot and wants to use the unsold vehicles as collateral for the loan. The bank has requested that his auditor (you) provide an audited listing of the vehicles' market values.

You have inventoried the cars and have verified that Joe Slimey is the actual owner of each of the cars. You have some questions, however, about the market value of some of the automobiles on the lot. Determine how much the automobiles are worth by searching the web.

Automobile	Features/Condition	Slimey's Valuation	Your Valuation
94 Dodge Caravan	Auto, A/C, AM/FM Cass., Cruise, Tilt	$8,900	
95 Pontiac Grand AM	Auto, A/C, AM/FM Stereo	$8,900	
94 Ford Crown Victoria	Auto, A/C, AM/FM Cass., PW, Cruise, Tilt	$11,900	
97 Chevy Camaro	V-6, Auto, A/C, Cruise, AM/FM Cass., Tilt	$15,900	
96 Pontiac Grand AM	Auto, A/C, AM/FM Cass. Power Locks	$10,900	
95 Chrysler New Yorker	Auto, A/C, AM/FM Cass., PW, PDI, Cruise, Tilt	$12,900	
95 Toyota Camry	Auto, A/C, AM/FM Cass., PW, PDI, Cruise, Tilt	$10,900	
94 Pontiac Grand Prix	Auto, A/C, AM/FM Cass., PW, PDI	$7,900	
96 Ford Full Size Pickup	Auto, A/C, AM/FM Cass., Bedliner	$12,900	
95 Dodge Caravan	Auto, A/C, AM/FM Cass., 7 Passenger	$9,900	

Here are some sites to verify used car prices:

Auto Pricing: **http://www.autopricing.com/**

Edmund's Automobile Buyer's Guides: **http://www.edmunds.com**

Kelley Blue Book: **http://www.kbb.com/**

Exercise 10.3: Existence

Big Time Sports sporting goods store is one of your largest clients. Management has expressed some concerns to you about the purchasing agent's improved life style--new car, new house, expensive clothes. They are concerned that his improved life style might be coming at the company's expense. While the confirmations that you have sent out to the company's vendors were returned without exception, whether or not they are *legitimate* vendors is another story. Following is a list of companies that have invoiced Big Time during the year. Perform a search on the Internet to verify that the vendor exists, that the address is correct, and that the vendor is an appropriate supplier of sporting goods products.

Vendor	Description of Business	Address	Comments
Alaska's Magnum Outfitters	Outdoor sporting goods	PO Box 202833 Anchorage, AL 99520	
Anchorshade	Large umbrellas for sports	1001 Jupiter Park Drive Suite 113 Jupiter, FL 33458	
Athletronics	Electronic sports cards and memorabilia	P.O. Box 231 Houston, TX 77204	
Avathar	Fishing equipment	PO Box 71118 Burlington, Ont. Canada	
Bike Chain	Specialized bicycles and accessories.	2721 Aborn Road Suite B San Jose, CA 95121	
Colorado Custom Rods	Custom fishing equipment	P.O. Box 712 Carbondale, CO 81623	
Myrt's Shop	Duck decoys	South Gouldsboro, ME 04607	
Reelman's Antique Fishing Tackle	Collectable fishing tackle	Rd 3 Box 481 Troy, PA 16947	
Shoe Business	Special purpose footwear	P.O. Box 231 Houston, TX 77204	
Shotmaker	Wholesales equipment for ice or roller hockey	Box 885 Baudette, MN 56623	
Victoria Skimboards	Surfing equipment	2955 Laguna Canyon Rd. Laguna Beach, CA 92651	

Hint: Some of these companies are real, some are not. Search the web to find websites for the real sporting goods suppliers.

Chapter 11: Production and Payroll Cycle

Exercise 11.1: Obtain Payroll Cycle Audit Program

The Internet provides a great deal of support for practicing accountants. For example, auditors often get together to share best practices. There are two sites that list audit programs for a number of different audit areas. If you need an audit program, you can simply access one of the sites, download a program, and modify it to meet the needs of your client's engagement.

Download a copy of an audit program that examines a client's Payroll cycle from one of the **Auditors Sharing Audit Programs (ASAP)** sites. Modify the program for use in the Kingston Company audit engagement.

Auditors Sharing Audit Programs (ASAP)

<u>http://users.aol.com/auditnet/asap_ind.htm</u>

or

<u>ftp.unf.edu/pub/auditnet/programs</u>

(**Note:** Do not use the "HTTP://" prefix when you attempt to access this site.)

(**Hint:** Be sure to read and study the background information about Kingston Company at the end of Chapter 4, the corporate minutes (5.18), and materials at the end of Chapter 6. You need to know about the company in order to <u>modify</u> an existing audit program. Do the best you can with the available information.)

Chapter 12: Finance and Investment Cycle

Examining investments is often one of the most critical audit areas in an audit engagement because of concerns over proper valuation. The Internet provides many resources, including audit programs and current and past security prices that enable the auditor to increase the efficiency and effectiveness. For example, we have listed some web sites that provide sources of daily stock market quotes.

APL Quotes: **http://www.secapl.com/cgi-bin/qs**

CNN Financial Network: **http://cnnfn.com**

Data Broadcasting Corporation: **http://www.dbc.com**

Interquote: **http://www.interquote.com/index.html**

PC Quotes: **http://www.pcquote.com**

Quotecom: **http://www.quote.com**

Quicken.com: **http://www.quicken.com/investments/quotes**

Exercise 12.1: Investment Portfolio Valuation

Below is a portfolio of marketable equity securities held by a company that is being considered for acquisition by one of your clients. As part of a merger and acquisition engagement, it is important to determine the current value of the potential acquiree's assets, including the current market price of its portfolio of marketable securities. Find the current stock prices for the investments below.

Investment	Symbol	Number of shares	Current Stock Price	Total Market Value
Exxon	XON	2000 shares		
Gillette	G	1100 shares		
Intel	INTC	1500 shares		
Johnson & Johnson	JNJ	1000 shares		
McDonalds	MCD	850 shares		
Merck	MRK	600 shares		
Microsoft	MSFT	1100 shares		
Minnesota Mining & Manufacturing	MMM	100 shares		
Total				

Exercise 12.2: Obtain Cycle Audit Program

The Internet provides a great deal of support for practicing accountants. For example, auditors often get together to share best practices. There are two sites that list audit programs for a number of different audit areas. If you need an audit program, you can simply access one of the sites, download a program, and modify it to meet the needs of your client's engagement.

Download a copy of an audit program that examines a client's investments from one of the **Auditors Sharing Audit Programs (ASAP)** sites. Modify the program for use in the Kingston Company audit engagement.

Auditors Sharing Audit Programs (ASAP)

http://users.aol.com/auditnet/asap_ind.htm

or

ftp.unf.edu/pub/auditnet/programs

(**Note:** Do not use the "HTTP://" prefix when you attempt to access this site.)

(**Hint:** Be sure to read and study the background information about Kingston Company at the end of Chapter 4, the corporate minutes (5.18), and materials at the end of Chapter 6. You need to know about the company in order to modify an existing audit program. Do the best you can with the available information.)

Chapter 13: Completing the Audit

Many business professionals have come to depend on the Internet for immediate notification of corporate events. Up-to-the-minute information, such as press releases and analyst announcements, are also available through free services, such as InfoBeat **(http://www.infobeat.com)** and PointCast **(http://www.pointcast.com)**. Additionally the following sites provide useful information on companies, the economy, and other events affecting the marketplace:

Source	Internet Site
CNN Financial Network	http://cnnfn.com
Department of Commerce	http://www.doc.gov
Disclosure Company	http://www.disclosure.com
Holt Report	http://metro.turnpike.net/holt/index.html
Hoovers on-line	http://www.hoovers.com
Investor Relations Web	http://www.investor-rel.com/index.html
Off-Line	http://www.off-on.com/top25.dbm
SEC's EDGAR Database	http://www.sec.gov/
TechWeb	http://www.techweb.com/
Wall Street Journal	http://interactive.wsj.com

Exercise 13.1: Search for Subsequent Events

Subsequent events, those issues or transactions that occur after a company's balance-sheet date but before the financial statements are issued, are an important part of the auditor's engagement. Choose a company that has a 12/31 year-end and download its audit report. (See Exercise 3.1 from Chapter 3) Do a search of the Internet resources listed above to identify significant transactions that occurred in the period between the fiscal year-end and the actual report issue date (on the auditor's report). Are there any issues that you believe should have been disclosed in the footnotes to the audit report? Return to the audited financial statements. Did the auditors require footnote disclosure for those items?

Module A: Test of Controls with Attribute Sampling

And

Module B: Test of Balances with Dollar Value Sampling

A partner in your firm doesn't have access to the Robertson and Louwers *Auditing* textbook and needs some additional training on current sampling methods. Given your excellent education, the partner has turned to you for advice on where to seek additional help. You would love to spend time discussing the costs and benefits of different methods of auditing sampling and when they should be used, but you are tied up on three separate audit engagements with three separate managers, each of whom believes that their audit is the most critical. Given your limited time, do a search on the Internet for resources on audit sampling available for training purposes. In a brief memo, list the books, courses, and seminars that would be available to the partner for study purposes. In your recommendations to the partner, include time, location, and cost considerations.

Module C: Auditing in an Electronic Environment

Computer Assisted Audit Tools (CAATS) are changing the way auditors perform their responsibilities, allowing them to complete their audits more effectively and more efficiently. Two of the most popular audit tools (ACL and IDEA) have web sites that allow guided tours and/or free product samples.

Exercise C.1: ACL Tutorial

ACL (short for Audit Command Language) is one of the leading providers of CAATs. Its site provides a brief tutorial of its product that allows you to see firsthand the strengths of computer assisted audit tools that are reshaping the auditing profession.

http://www.acl.com/

Exercise C.2: IDEA

IDEA (Interactive Data Extraction and Analysis), developed by the Canadian Institute of Chartered Accountants, is one of the leading Computer Assisted Audit Tools (CAATs) for the auditing profession. The IDEA site allows you to order a CD-ROM demonstration version of IDEA to "test-drive." This will enable you to experience first-hand one of the CAATs that is allowing auditors to perform their audits more *efficiently* **and** *effectively*.

Canadian Institute of Chartered Accountants (CICA)

http://www.cica.ca/idea/index.htm/

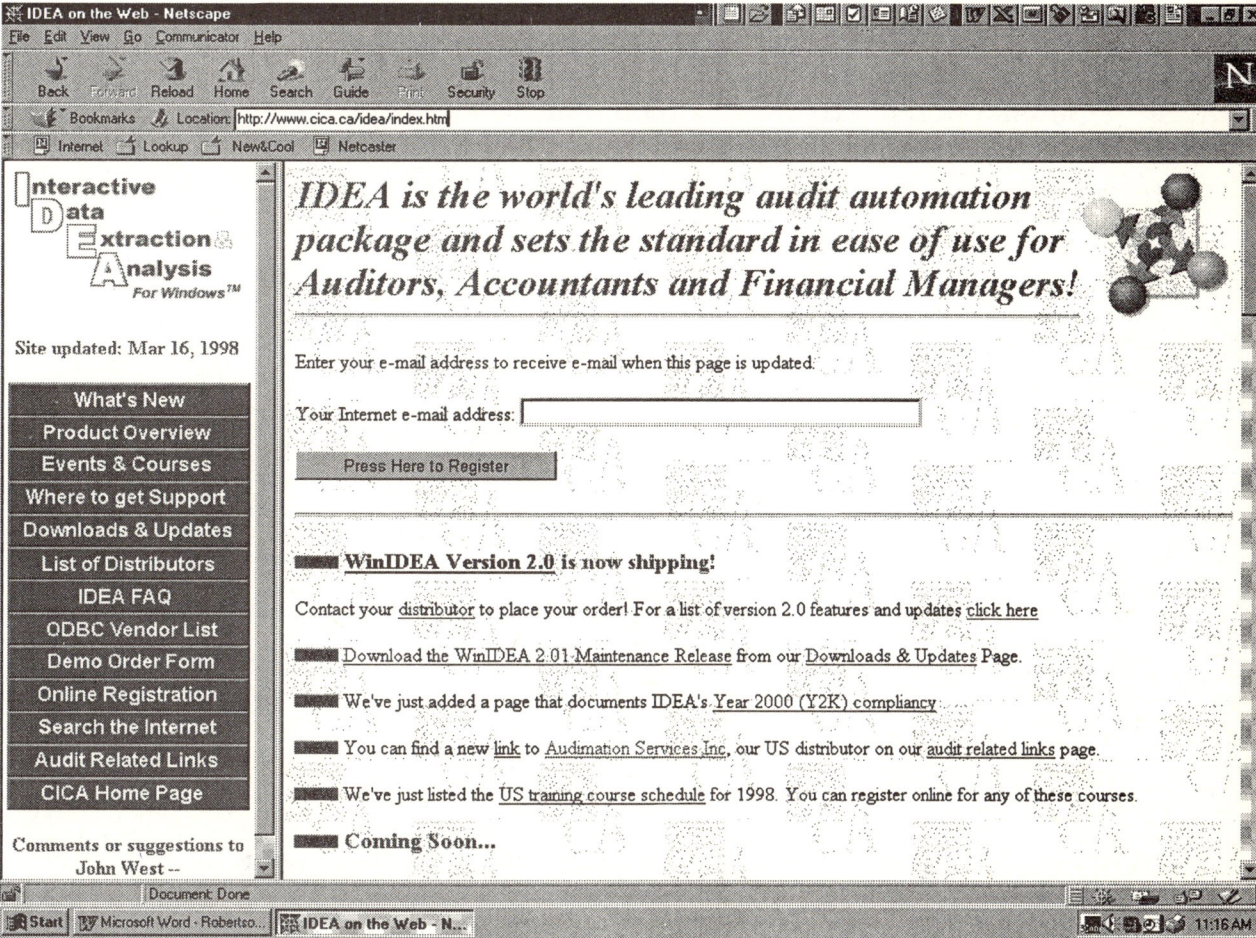

Permission to include the page image of the IDEA website was obtained from the CICA.

Module D: Information System Auditing

As you can see by the exercises that you have done so far, the Internet is used for a number of practical purposes. The Internet is also being abused--some examples of Internet abuse include:

1. Software piracy.

2. Computer systems break ins ("hacking")

3. Theft of private information

4. Contamination of private information resources

5. Commercial theft

6. Transmission of sexually explicit materials

Exercise D.1: Internet Security

Here are some Internet Security-Related sites. Visit these sites to find the latest on Internet security.

http://www-ns.rutgers.edu/www-security/index.html

http://www.alw.nih.gov/Security/security.html

http://csrc.ncsl.nist.gov/first/

http://www.cis.ohio-state.edu/hypertext/faq/usenet/firewalls-faq/faq.html

http://csrc.ncsl.nist.gov/

http://www.2600.com/

http://www.sei.cmu.edu/SEI/programs/cert/CERT.info.html

file://info.cert.org/pub/

Exercise D.2: Internet Security Incidents

Several highly publicized Internet security incidents have occurred over the past several years. Do a search to find additional information on one or more of the incidents or Internet abuses below.

- "Morris worm"
- Chaos Club, WANK, Legion of Doom "hacker" clubs
- Data capture/data intercept
- IP "spoofing"
- French government accused of espionage
- Wire transfer theft of money from Citicorp
- Yahoo site hacked!
- USA Today site hacked!
- Department of Defense site hacked!
- NASA site hacked!

Write a brief memo documenting your findings. Include in your memo the following items:

1. What happened?

2. How did it occur?

3. How can it be prevented from occurring to your company or one of your clients in the future?

Module E: Other Public Accounting Services and Reports

Assignment E.1: CPA WebTrust

The AICPA recently launched a new assurance service entitled CPA WebTrust.

http://www.aicpa.org

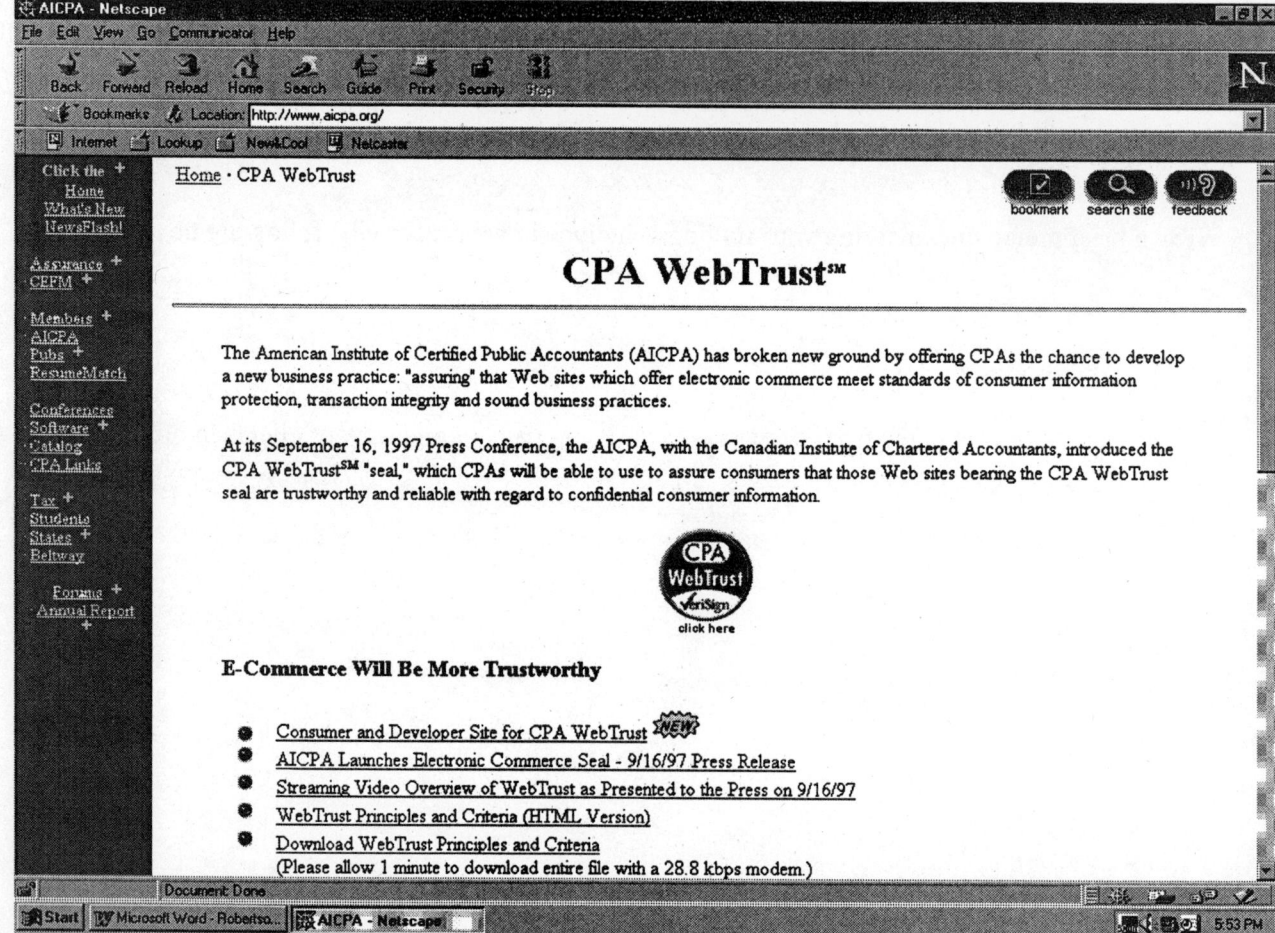

Access the AICPA web site to answer the following questions:

1. What is WebTrust?

Permission to include the image of the AICPA WebTrust website was obtained from the AICPA.

Exercise E.1 (Continued)

2. Why is WebTrust needed?

3. How does an Internet user know that a website has received the WebTrust service?

4. Where can a person obtain copies of the WebTrust standards?

5. Does the WebTrust seal cover security and privacy of the Internet Service Provider (ISP) that hosts a website?

Module F: Operational Auditing: Governmental and Internal Audits

Listed below are some websites for learning more about internal auditing and governmental auditing. Check out the sites below before answering the questions on the following pages.

Internal Audit Web Sites

The Internal Auditing WWW
http://www.bitwise.net/iawww/

Institute of Internal Auditors (IIA)
http://www.theiia.org/

Governmental Audit Web Sites

Association of College and University Auditors (ACUA) Homepage
http://www.acua.org

Government Auditor's Resource Page
http://www.infi.net/~zsudiak/GARP.html

Governmental Accounting Office (GAO)
http://www.gao.gov/

Exercise F.1: CIA Certification

The IIA web site lists the requirements to a Certified Internal Auditor (CIA). The site also lists questions and answers from recent CIA examinations. Visit the IIA site and answer the following questions:

http://www.theiia.org/

1. What are the requirements for becoming a CIA?

2. When are the next CIA exam dates?

3. Do you need a college degree in order to sit for the CIA exam? In other words, can a person take the CIA before graduating from college?

Take the 48 questions on the interactive CIA exam. How did you do?

Exercise F.2: The GAO: It's not just a job

Visit the GAO web site and find out more about the Governmental Accounting Office.

Governmental Accounting Office (GAO)

http://www.gao.gov/

1. What is the GAO and what is its mission?

2. Access the 1997 Consolidated Financial Statements of the United States Government. What kind of opinion did the government receive?

3. What kinds of job opportunities does the GAO offer?

Module G: Professional Ethics

Exercise G.1: AICPA Code of Professional Conduct

The AICPA's Code of Professional Conduct is on the Web! Visit the AICPA's site to determine whether the following scenarios violate the AICPA's Code of Professional Conduct. Cite the specific section in the Code to support your answers.

http://www.aicpa.org

	Scenario	Violation of the AICPA Code of Professional Conduct? (Yes or No)	Citation in Code
1.	CPA Josephine E. is a manager in the Houston office of J&T, CPAs LLP. She owns 100 Class B Woodcraft Company common shares (out of 1,000,000 shares outstanding). The Woodcraft audit is performed by the J&T office in Chicago.		
2.	CPA Marcus E. obtained a $120,000 home loan from Megabank in 1986. The loan was made under normal lending procedures, terms, and requirements, and is secured by a first lien on the house. Marcus has worked on the Megabank audit team since 1985.		
3.	CPA Sarah E. tried many ways to build her accounting practice. Recently she paid a BusinessANEW (a "client search firm") $2,000 for each new client BusinessANEW brought to her office. Sara's standard engagement letter for all new clients tells about her relationship with BusinessANEW and the $2,000 per-client payment		
4.	CPA J. Earp wrote in a promotional letter sent to his firm's clients: "When I make a presentation to the Tombstone County tax equity hearing board, the chair always sees it my way."		
5.	CPA Wyatt E. works on the Megabank audit team and has in the bank a regular checking account fully insured by the FDIC (i.e., less than $100,000 balance).		
6.	CPA Morgan E. is a 30% owner of the JH Holiday CPA firm that audits the Klondike Casino Company. Morgan owns 15% of the common stock of Klondike and is very aware of the AICPA independence rules that prohibit this kind of financial interest. To solve the problem and provide college funds for six children, Morgan carefully arranged for the stock to be held in a blind trust that discloses no information about trust assets or activities to the Morgan E. family.		
7.	CPA Warren E. owns the Landmark One office building and leases the entire building to BigRealty Company for a $1 million annual payment. BigRealty serves as agent and subleases space to commercial tenants. Warren stays informed about this material investment through information obtained as the auditor of BigRealty's financial statements.		
8.	CPA Virgil E. performed actuarial consulting services for The Clanton Insurance Company and billed Clanton in the amount of $150,000 in March eighteen months ago. Now Virgil is about to complete the Clanton financial statement audit for Clanton's fiscal year ended on June 30 by writing an unqualified audit report.		

Exercise G.2: State Board of Accountancy Codes of Professional Conduct

While the AICPA Code of Professional Conduct is widely accepted, CPAs also must follow the laws and regulations of their state legislatures and state boards of accountancy. Go to the NASBA site (address below) to find information about the laws and regulations in your state.

http://www.nasba.org

Choose two (2) states of interest to you. Compare some of the regulations for similarities and differences. Write a two-page memo describing your comparison.

Module H: Legal Liability

One of the great resources on the World Wide Web for auditors is the SEC's EDGAR system. EDGAR stands for Electronic Data Gathering, Analysis and Retrieval System. Most of the documents filed with the SEC are filed electronically and are available on the SEC's web page. Access the SEC's web page and answer the following questions:

http://www.sec.gov/

Exercise H.1: Form Filing Requirements

List the filing requirements for the following SEC forms. Describe any responsibility that an auditor may have in the filing process.

Form	Filing Requirements: Who must file and when?
Form ADV-S	
Form BD	
Form S-1	
Form SB-1	
Form 8-K	
Form 10-K	
Form 10-Q	
Form 12b-25	

Exercise H.2: Auditor's Legal Liability

The SEC recently (April 16, 1997) released a report describing the impact of the Private Securities Litigation Reform Act of 1995 ("the Act") on the nature and extent of securities-related litigation. Access the SEC's report to the President and Congress and summarize the SEC's major findings below.

http://www.sec.gov/

Has the number of companies sued in federal court as a result of securities class actions increased or decreased since the passage of the Act? What are the possible reasons for the change?

Is it more or less difficult for plaintiffs to bring and prosecute securities class action lawsuits?

Has the Act affected the number of state filings of securities class actions?

Are secondary defendants, such as accountants and lawyers, being named more or less frequently in securities class actions?

Have the provisions of the Act encouraged companies to provide more forward-looking disclosures beyond what they provided prior to enactment of Act? Why or why not?

Appendix A: Other Cool Stuff

NetMind's URL-minder

URL-minder sends you e-mail notification when your favorite accounting Web pages change. URL-minder is a free service that you can use to monitor any public Web pages on the Internet. You can register as many pages as you like.

http://minder.netmind.com/URL-minder/

Cool Internet DOS Commands

Tracert. To find how many relay points exist between your computer and your favorite web site, enter the following command at a DOS prompt:

tracert <web site address>

You should see a list of the sites that information must pass through before it gets to you.

Ping. If a web site appears to be down, you can check the site by typing the following command at a DOS prompt:

ping <web site address>

If the site is active, information will be sent from your computer to the site. If the site doesn't respond, there is something wrong along the way.

Appendix B: Other Auditing Web Sites

Auditing Resources

American Accounting Association Auditing Section's Web Site
http://www.indiana.edu/~audsec/index.html

Accounting Net http://www.accountingnet.com

A-Net: Links to the World http://www.csu.edu.au/index.html

Auditing and Accounting Resources Site Seeker http://www.kentis.com/auditacc.html

AuditNet http://users.aol.com/auditnet/

Canadian Institute of Chartered Accountants http://www.cica.ca/

Rutgers Accounting Web (RAW) http://www.rutgers.edu/Accounting

Accounting and Consulting Firms

Arthur Andersen http://www.ArthurAndersen.com

Andersen Consulting http://www.ac.com

Associated Accounting Firms International Network http://www.accountingnet.com/asso/aafi

Auditforce http://www.auditforce.com

BDO Seidman http://www.bdo.com

Coopers & Lybrand http://www.colybrand.com

CorpFiNet Directory of Accounting Firms http://www.corpfinet.com/Accounting.html

Deloitte and Touche http://www.dttus.com

Ernst & Young http://www.ey.com

Grant Thornton http://www.gt.com

KPMG http://www.us.kpmg.com

Price Waterhouse http://www.pw.com